T0395710

MAP
YOUR PLANET

NATURAL DISASTERS

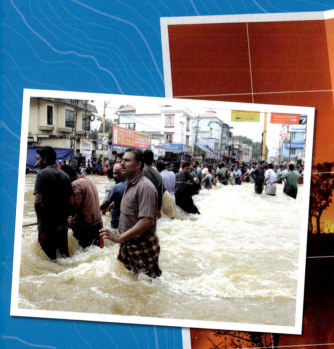

RACHEL MINAY

Cavendish
Square

Published in 2024 by Cavendish Square Publishing, LLC
2544 Clinton Street, Buffalo, NY 14224

Website: cavendishsq.com

This publication represents the opinions and views of the author based on his or her personal experience, knowledge, and research. The information in this book serves as a general guide only. The author and publisher have used their best efforts in preparing this book and disclaim liability rising directly or indirectly from the use and application of this book.

All websites were available and accurate when this book was sent to press.

Editor: Rachel Minay
Series designer: Rocket Design (East Anglia) Ltd

The publisher would like to thank the following for permission to reproduce their pictures:
Alamy: Nelly George 19(t), Xinhua 20(b), Alex MacNaughton 21(cl), Majority World CIC 26(b), ZUMA Press Inc. 27(t), Xinhua 28(c); NASA (NASA Earth Observatory image by Joshua Stevens, using data from the Famine Early Warning Systems Network (FEWS NET) and the U.S. Geological Survey) 23(t); Shutterstock: AJP cover (inset), Tongra239 cover (main), Lysogor Roman 4(c), Peter Hermes Furian 4(b), Sangoiri 5, Wead 6, Imon 7(t), Alexander Piragis 7(b), Darryl Brooks 8(c), JethroT 8(b), Morphart Creation 9(t), valipatov 9(b), think4photop 10(c), Varunyuuu 10(b), Fajrul Islam 11(t), fiki j bhayangkara 11(b), Frans Delian 12(b), Stefano Ember 13(t), Rasica 14(t), Pipochka 14(b), aapsky 15(t), Terry Kelly 15(b), arindambanerjee 16(c), elRoce 17(t), arindambanerjee 17(b), AJP 18(c), matrioshka 18(b), Wei Huang 19(b), Michel Kluyskens 21(cr), Sadik Gulek 22(b), SkycopterFilms Archives 23(b), Ecopix 24(cr), John Carnemolla 24(bl), Alex Cimbal 25(c), barmalini 27(bl), Kirill Chernyshev 27(br), Pyty 28–29, JULIAN LOTT 28(b), Talukdar David 29(t), Anna LoFi 29(b).
Design elements by Shutterstock.
Map illustrations: Julian Baker: 8–9, 12–13, 16–17, 20–21, 24–25.

Cataloging-in-Publication Data

Names: Minay, Rachel.
Title: Natural disasters / Rachel Minay.
Description: New York : Cavendish Square Publishing, 2024. | Series: Map your planet | Includes glossary and index.
Identifiers: ISBN 9781502668509 (pbk.) | ISBN 9781502668516 (library bound) | ISBN 9781502668523 (ebook)
Subjects: LCSH: Natural disasters--Juvenile literature.
Classification: LCC GB5019.M563 2024 | DDC 363.34078--dc23

CPSIA compliance information: Batch #CSCSQ24:
For further information contact Cavendish Square Publishing LLC at 1-877-980-4450.

Printed in the United States of America

Find us on

CONTENTS

What is a natural disaster? 4

Volcanoes 6

Mapping Vesuvius 8

Earthquakes and tsunamis 10

Mapping the 2004 Indian Ocean tsunami   12

Extreme weather 14

Mapping Haiti 16

Floods 18

Mapping East Africa 20

Droughts 22

Mapping southeastern Australia 24

People and natural disasters 26

Mapping climate disasters 28

Glossary 30

Further information 31

Index 32

WHAT IS A
NATURAL DISASTER?

Natural disasters are often sudden events that cause serious damage or loss of life. As the name suggests, they have natural causes – but they can also be linked to human activity.

HAZARDS

Natural hazards are extreme events caused by the Earth's processes. When these events affect people in a bad way, they are called natural disasters. Most are related to tectonics or to the weather.

An avalanche is when a mass of snow falls down a mountainside. Avalanches can be triggered by natural causes or by people.

TECTONIC HAZARDS

Earth's crust is made up of moving pieces called tectonic plates. The place where two plates meet is called a plate boundary. Volcanoes (see pages 6–7) and earthquakes (see pages 10–11) are natural hazards that usually occur at these boundaries.

MAP MASTERS

From the 1950s, improvements in technology have made it easier to map the ocean floor, leading to better understanding about tectonics. Maps that show tectonic plates have existed only since then.

Eurasian Plate

Pacific Plate

North American Plate

Indian Plate

African Plate

South American Plate

Australian Plate

Antarctic Plate

WEATHER HAZARDS

Weather hazards include severe storms, tornadoes and blizzards (see pages 14–15), floods (see pages 18–19), and droughts (see pages 22–23).

CLIMATE CHANGE

There have always been times when extreme weather leads to natural disasters. However, many scientists think climate change is making some disasters more frequent and more severe.

Natural disasters have natural causes, but they can be affected by human activities, such as those that cause climate change.

VOLCANOES

A volcano is an opening in the Earth's crust that allows magma, gases, and ash to escape from within the Earth. Volcanoes often occur at plate boundaries, where tectonic plates are moving away from or under each other.

TYPES OF VOLCANOES

The two main types of volcanoes are stratovolcanoes, which are steep-sided and cone-shaped, and shield volcanoes, which have gently sloping sides. Volcanoes can be active, dormant, or extinct.

ERUPTIONS

Magma is hot molten (melted) rock under the Earth's crust. When a volcano erupts, magma comes out as lava, along with gas and ash. Eruptions often cause deadly pyroclastic flows – very hot, very fast avalanches of gas, ash, and rock.

Mount Etna in Sicily, Italy, is one of the world's most active stratovolcanoes.

This map shows the "Ring of Fire" – an imaginary line around the Pacific Ocean where the Pacific Plate meets other tectonic plates. This is where most of the world's volcanic eruptions and earthquakes occur.

Ring of Fire

FACT

THE RING OF FIRE IS HOME TO ABOUT 75 PERCENT OF EARTH'S VOLCANOES AND 90 PERCENT OF ITS EARTHQUAKES.

Around one in every 15 people lives in an area at risk from an active volcano.

VIOLENT VOLCANOES

Some of the world's deadliest eruptions have been in Indonesia, which is within the Ring of Fire. They include:

Toba – a supervolcanic eruption about 75,000 years ago. Some scientists think it caused a massive global winter and pushed humans toward extinction.

Tambora, 1815 – the most powerful eruption in recorded history. It had global effects, including the "year without a summer" (1816), which led to massive food shortages.

Krakatoa, 1883 and **Anak Krakatoa ("Child of Krakatoa"), 2018** – both caused devastating tsunamis (see page 11).

MAPPING
VESUVIUS

Mount Vesuvius is a volcano near Naples in Italy. A violent eruption in CE 79 caused a terrible natural disaster – one that has been "frozen" in time.

❶ VESUVIUS

The eruption of Mount Vesuvius in CE 79 is one of the most famous in history. It started when a gigantic cloud of ash, rock, and gas exploded into the air. This blocked out the sun, and volcanic ash and rock rained down.

❷ POMPEII

The nearby town of Pompeii was covered in ash, but worse was to come. Super-heated pyroclastic flows rushed down the volcano, devastating Pompeii and killing people instantly.

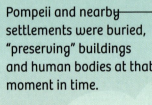

Pompeii and nearby settlements were buried, "preserving" buildings and human bodies at that moment in time.

❸ HERCULANEUM

Herculaneum was a small wealthy town that was also destroyed and buried by the eruption. It lay hidden under 66 feet (20 m) of volcanic ash and rock until the eighteenth century.

Like Pompeii, Herculaneum was preserved almost intact.

4 TODAY

Many people live near Vesuvius today. The volcano is closely monitored and around 800,000 people will be evacuated if there is an eruption warning.

4 Naples

3 Herculaneum

1 Mount Vesuvius

2 Pompeii

ITALY

Bay of Naples

Mediterranean Sea

● = Cities destroyed

VESUVIUS: ITALY

MAP MASTERS

Vesuvius has erupted many times. This nineteenth-century map shows the spread of lava from an eruption in 1631.

EARTHQUAKES
AND TSUNAMIS

Earthquakes cause some of the most catastrophic natural disasters. Both earthquakes and volcanoes can also trigger huge sea waves called tsunamis.

EARTHQUAKES

Like volcanoes, earthquakes often happen at plate boundaries. The moving plates sometimes become stuck, but because they are still trying to move, pressure builds up. Eventually, the pressure becomes so great that it is released as a rapid flow of energy through the Earth. The point directly above this on the surface is called the epicenter of the earthquake. The main earthquake can be followed by smaller earthquakes called aftershocks.

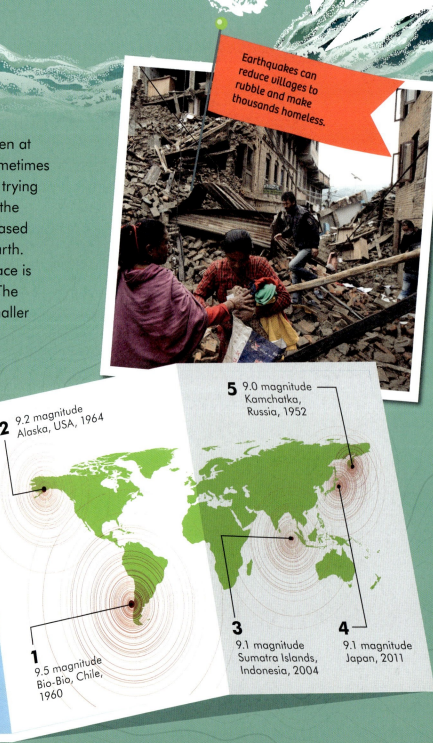

Earthquakes can reduce villages to rubble and make thousands homeless.

MAP MASTERS

This map shows the location and magnitude (size or strength) of the five biggest earthquakes since 1900.

2 9.2 magnitude Alaska, USA, 1964

5 9.0 magnitude Kamchatka, Russia, 1952

1 9.5 magnitude Bio-Bio, Chile, 1960

3 9.1 magnitude Sumatra Islands, Indonesia, 2004

4 9.1 magnitude Japan, 2011

TSUNAMIS

Tsunamis are massive sea waves. They are sometimes called "tidal waves," but they have nothing to do with tides. A tsunami happens when something – for example an underwater earthquake or volcanic eruption – causes a large volume of water to be displaced (spread out across the sea).

Tsunamis can be devastating to coastal communities.

Earthquakes sometimes cause soil, which is a solid, to behave like a liquid, which means buildings sink. This is what happened on the Indonesian island of Sulawesi in 2018.

FACT

TSUNAMIS ARE FRIGHTENINGLY FAST. THEY CAN TRAVEL THOUSANDS OF MILES AT SPEEDS OF UP TO 500 MILES (800 KM) PER HOUR.

EARTH-SHATTERING EFFECTS

Earthquakes cause the ground to shake and split apart. They can also lead to landslides, fires, and floods. Both earthquakes and tsunamis can cause damage to buildings and loss of life.

MAPPING THE 2004 INDIAN OCEAN TSUNAMI

The deadliest tsunami in history was in the Indian Ocean in 2004. It was caused by a massive undersea earthquake.

The tsunami affected all the countries shown on this map, with major damage and loss of life in Indonesia, Sri Lanka, India, and Thailand.

1 EARTHQUAKE

On December 26, 2004, an earthquake with a magnitude of 9.1–9.3 occurred. Its epicenter was just off the west coast of northern Sumatra in Indonesia, close to places where lots of people lived. The earthquake caused a tsunami with waves up to 100 feet (30 m) high.

2 INDONESIA

The tsunami hit Indonesia about 20 minutes after the earthquake. Around 1,500 villages were destroyed in northern Sumatra and at least 130,000 people were killed.

Banda Aceh, a major city in northern Sumatra, was hardest hit by the tsunami.

Somalia

Kenya

Seychelles

Tanzania

Madagasgar

3 SRI LANKA

The tsunami hit Sri Lanka about two hours after the earthquake, causing over 35,000 deaths.

The tsunami destroyed around 60 percent of Sri Lanka's fishing boats, so it had a big effect on people's livelihoods.

Bangladesh

India

Burma

Thailand

3

Maldives

Sri Lanka

1

2

Malaysia

epicenter

Indonesia

Indian Ocean

TSUNAMI: INDIAN OCEAN

FACT

THE TSUNAMI CAUSED 230,000 DEATHS AND LEFT 1.7 MILLION PEOPLE HOMELESS.

WARNING SYSTEM

The 2004 tsunami was particularly bad because people had little or no warning. A tsunami warning system for the Indian Ocean has now been set up.

EXTREME WEATHER

Extreme weather, including wind, snow, rain, and drought, can cause different kinds of natural disasters.

TORNADOES

Tornadoes form where a warm wind meets a cold one. A rapidly spinning column of air drops out of a thunder cloud toward the ground.

FACT

THE WORST TORNADOES CAN BE HUNDREDS OF FEET WIDE, DESTROY BUILDINGS, AND THROW OBJECTS SUCH AS CARS OVER 320 FEET (100 M).

BLIZZARDS

Blizzards are strong snowstorms with high winds. The deadliest blizzard in history was in Iran in 1972. It buried 200 villages and left 4,000 people dead.

For a true-life story of what may have been the worst-ever winter in the U.S., turn to page 31.

TROPICAL STORMS

Tropical storms have different names in different parts of the world, including hurricanes, typhoons, and cyclones. They start over oceans in tropical areas and build up energy there, with winds whirling in a circle. The heavy rainfall and strong winds they bring when they reach land can cause floods and mudslides.

 **MAP MASTERS**

It's hard to predict the path of a tropical storm, but specialist forecasting centers try to do just this so that they can warn people who might be affected. They detect and track storms using satellites, weather instruments, and computer modeling, while special aircraft fly over and through storms to collect data.

In 2018, around 500,000 people were ordered to evacuate ahead of Hurricane Michael. The storm caused severe damage, particularly in Florida.

MAPPING
HAITI

Haiti is
It

① EARTHQUAKE, 2010

In 2010, Haiti suffered one of the deadliest earthquakes of all time. The epicenter of the earthquake was 15.5 miles (25 km) west of Port-au-Prince, the country's capital.

Homes, businesses, and other buildings, such as hospitals, collapsed. Haiti is a low-income country and had very few earthquake-resistant buildings.

Caribbean Sea

Haiti is a country on the island of Hispaniola in the Caribbean.

②

HAITI: CARIBBEAN

FACT

ESTIMATES VARY, BUT THE 2010 EARTHQUAKE MAY HAVE CAUSED OVER 220,000 DEATHS AND MADE 1.3 MILLION PEOPLE HOMELESS.

② HURRICANE MATTHEW, 2016

Just six years after the terrible earthquake, a category 5 hurricane (the strongest on the scale) hit Haiti. It caused 546 deaths and affected over a million people, with 200,000 homes destroyed.

Hurricane Matthew caused a humanitarian crisis in Haiti, but the storm itself made it hard for emergency aid to reach people.

Atlantic Ocean

HISPANIOLA

HAITI

Dominican Republic

① Port-au-Prince

epicenter

③ CHOLERA, 2010S

Natural disasters sometimes lead to other kinds of disasters, such as epidemics. Cholera is an often-fatal infectious disease that is now rare in many parts of the world because of improved sanitation. The first modern large-scale outbreak followed the 2010 earthquake – the first case in Haiti in over a century quickly spread to the rest of the country.

Some hospitals collapsed after the Haiti earthquake. These health workers had to work in a makeshift tent, making their job even more challenging.

FLOODS

A flood is when water overflows onto land that is usually dry. Floods can be caused by heavy rain or snowmelt, or by surges from tropical storms.

CAUSES

Floods are caused by heavy or long periods of rain, or when mountain ice and snow melt rapidly. Rivers and other waterways become so full that they "break their banks," spilling onto the surrounding land. Storm surges are coastal floods that occur as a result of storms with high winds.

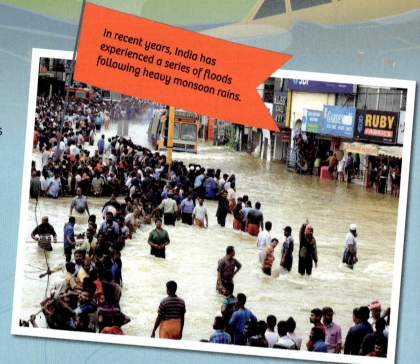

In recent years, India has experienced a series of floods following heavy monsoon rains.

EFFECTS

Floods can cause fatalities, as well as widespread damage, for example to power and water supplies, roads, farmland, and buildings. However, floods can sometimes have positive effects. Some ancient civilizations, including the Egyptians and the Indus Valley Civilization, flourished on the banks of flood-prone rivers.

The ancient Egyptians depended on the annual flooding of the Nile. It made fertile soil that helped crops grow.

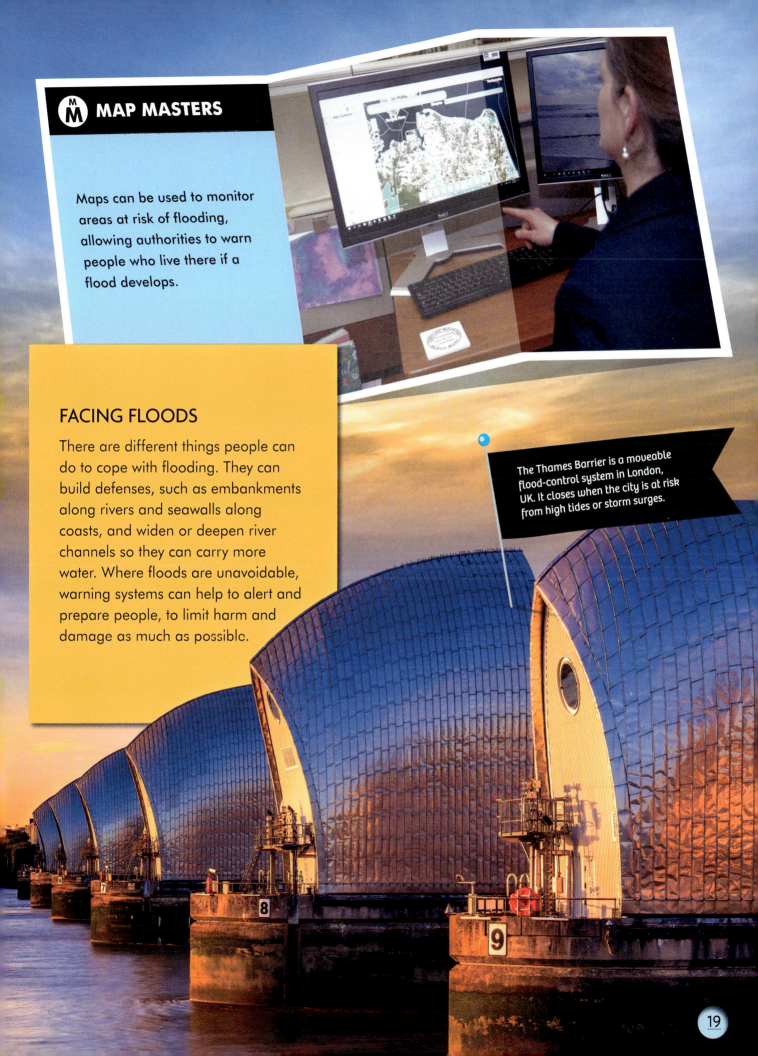

MAP MASTERS

Maps can be used to monitor areas at risk of flooding, allowing authorities to warn people who live there if a flood develops.

FACING FLOODS

There are different things people can do to cope with flooding. They can build defenses, such as embankments along rivers and seawalls along coasts, and widen or deepen river channels so they can carry more water. Where floods are unavoidable, warning systems can help to alert and prepare people, to limit harm and damage as much as possible.

The Thames Barrier is a moveable flood-control system in London, UK. It closes when the city is at risk from high tides or storm surges.

MAPPING
EAST AFRICA

East Africa had severe floods in both 2018 and 2020. They affected a number of countries, but in both cases Kenya and Rwanda were hardest hit.

DROUGHT TO DELUGE

In 2018, unusually heavy rains followed a year of severe drought. You might think that a lot of rain after a drought is a good thing, but the opposite can be true. If too much rain falls too quickly on land that has been baked dry and lost vegetation, the land cannot absorb it, increasing the chance of flooding.

Floods in 2020 affected hundreds of thousands of Kenyans, including many who were forced to leave their homes.

Other East African countries affected by floods in 2018 and 2020 include Somalia, Burundi, Djibouti, Ethiopia, and Uganda.

Sudan

Eritrea

Djibouti

Ethiopia

South Sudan

1

Uganda

Kenya

2

Rwanda

Burundi

Congo

Tanzania

Zambia

DOUBLE DISASTERS

Very heavy rainfall can lead to more than one type of natural disaster. As the ground on hills or mountains is saturated with water, it can become unstable and cause terrible landslides and mudslides.

① KENYA

Floods, mudslides, and buildings collapsing caused at least 186 deaths in Kenya in 2018 — 48 people were killed when a dam burst. In 2020, the death toll was even higher, at 237.

As many as 2.5 million people live in slums in Kenya's capital, Nairobi. Natural disasters can make life for people living in already challenging conditions even worse.

② RWANDA

Hilly countries like Rwanda are at particular risk of landslides. At least 200 people died in 2018 and 97 in 2020 as a result of floods, landslides, and mudslides.

Rwanda is sometimes called the "land of a thousand hills." This mountainous terrain means it is vulnerable to landslides and mudslides.

EAST AFRICA

DROUGHTS

A drought is a long period of dry weather. Because they affect water supply and food production, droughts can have terrible consequences.

CAUSES

Droughts are caused by a severe water shortage. They are natural, because they are a regular feature of the climate in many parts of the world. However, human activities, such as cutting down trees and building dams, can also contribute to droughts.

PRECIOUS WATER

Water is a basic human need and a precious resource. We all need clean water to drink, as well as for washing, cleaning, and cooking. Food production also depends on crops and livestock getting enough water. Droughts lead to both thirst and hunger, risking lives. They can cause people to leave their home country on a mass scale, which in turn puts pressure on neighboring countries.

East Africa suffered a severe drought during 2011 and 2012. A food crisis in Somalia led to many refugees fleeing to Kenya and Ethiopia, countries that were also affected by drought.

MAP MASTERS

Satellite mapping combined with data can track changes in average rainfall. This can help predict where crops may fail and therefore help to warn and reduce risk of famine.

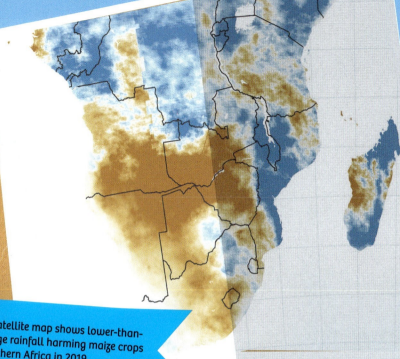

This satellite map shows lower-than-average rainfall harming maize crops in southern Africa in 2019.

DANGEROUS DROUGHTS

Unlike many natural disasters, droughts are not sudden but can last for months or even years. People need clean water for basic hygiene as well as drinking, so droughts can lead to the spread of disease. Other negative effects include an increase in wildfires, soil erosion, and desertification – these all reduce plant life, which in turn means less water evaporating from plants and so less rainfall.

We all need a safe and reliable water supply, but around one in every ten people doesn't have access to clean water.

MAPPING SOUTHEASTERN AUSTRALIA

From 2001 to 2009, Australia experienced the '"Millennium drought," the country's worst drought in well over a century.

1 ## MURRAY-DARLING BASIN

The worst-affected area was around the Murray and Darling Rivers. Home to nearly 2 million people, this region supplies most of Australia's water and much of its food.

2 ## IMPACTS

The drought had a serious impact on farming and therefore people's livelihoods. Crops and livestock were lost. The drought also damaged the soil, which affected future farming.

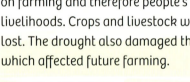

Droughts affect animals as well as people. Livestock suffers, but so do natural ecosystems. Rivers dry up and wildfires destroy habitats.

FACT

THE MURRAY-DARLING BASIN USUALLY SUPPLIES 75 PERCENT OF THE COUNTRY'S WATER AND 40 PERCENT OF ITS AGRICULTURAL PRODUCE.

Pacific
Ocean

SOUTH EASTERN AUSTRALIA

Queensland

Darling River

Brisbane ●

1

Murray–Darling Basin

2

New South Wales

Sydney ●

Murray River

Canberra ●

Victoria

3

● Melbourne

Tasmania

RESPONSES

The Australian government made some big changes to manage water supplies for the future, including building six major desalination plants between 2006 and 2012. Desalination is purifying salty seawater so people can drink it or use it to water crops.

Desalination plants, like this one in Melbourne, are an expensive but possible solution to water shortages.

PEOPLE AND NATURAL DISASTERS

The word "natural" in natural disasters tells us that they are a part of life on Earth. But does our behavior affect them — and is there anything we can do about them?

CLIMATE CHANGE

Although natural disasters are not caused by people, human activities can make them worse or more likely, particularly activities that cause climate change. We have always had weather disasters, such as droughts and tropical storms, but these have become more frequent and destructive in recent years and many scientists agree that this is linked to climate change.

POVERTY AND DISASTERS

Natural disasters can affect anyone, but it is the poorest people who suffer most. High-income countries are more able to afford solutions, such as warning systems and flood defenses. However, these countries also create more of the greenhouse gases that lead to global warming. Lower-income countries contribute less to climate change, but are hardest hit by natural disasters.

Natural disasters can cause people to lose their homes and livelihoods, face food and water shortages, and put their health at risk.

FACT

PEOPLE IN LOWER-INCOME COUNTRIES ARE FOUR TIMES MORE LIKELY TO BE DISPLACED BY EXTREME WEATHER THAN PEOPLE IN HIGHER-INCOME COUNTRIES.

LIVING WITH HAZARDS

Natural hazards exist, but we can try to avoid them becoming disasters. Risk can be reduced by using early warning systems, planning for evacuation, and by designing buildings that can withstand extreme events. Climate-related disasters are everyone's responsibility – we all need to work together to tackle the climate crisis.

These children are practicing how to protect themselves during an earthquake.

BENEFITS

Some natural hazards – such as earthquakes – only have negative effects, but others have some benefits for the people who live with them.

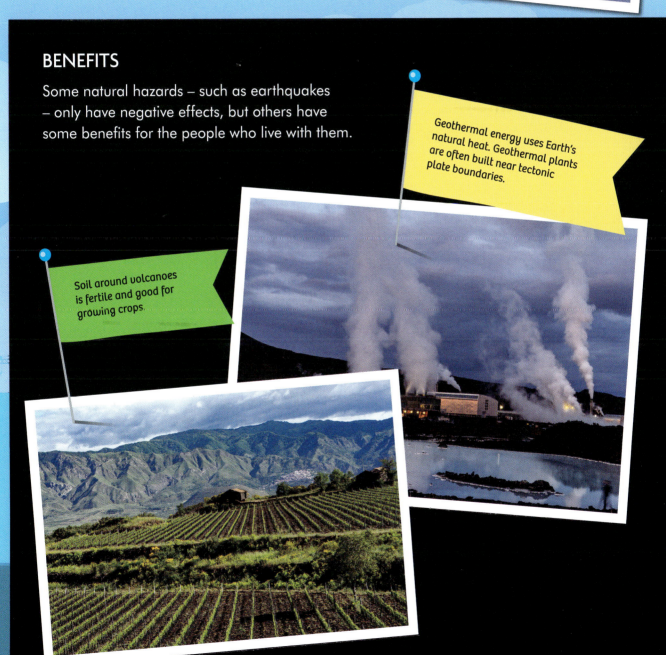

Geothermal energy uses Earth's natural heat. Geothermal plants are often built near tectonic plate boundaries.

Soil around volcanoes is fertile and good for growing crops.

MAPPING
CLIMATE DISASTERS

It is hard to link climate change to specific natural disasters. However, scientists are increasingly able to say that climate change makes some extreme weather both more frequent and more destructive.

❶

CENTRAL AMERICA

2019 was the fifth straight year of drought in Central American countries such as Guatemala and Honduras. Crop failure meant 3.5 million people needed humanitarian help.

Severe drought has devastated this Guatemalan farmer's corn crop.

❷

SOUTHEASTERN AFRICA

In March 2019, Cyclone Idai caused 1,300 deaths in Mozambique, Zimbabwe, and Malawi. Just a month later, Mozambique was hit by Cyclone Kenneth, the strongest to hit the country since records began.

This map looks at some recent natural disasters related to the climate.

NORTH AMERICA

❶

SOUTH AMERICA

A cyclone destroyed this house in Malawi.

FACT

CLIMATE-RELATED DISASTERS HAVE TRIPLED OVER THE LAST 30 YEARS.

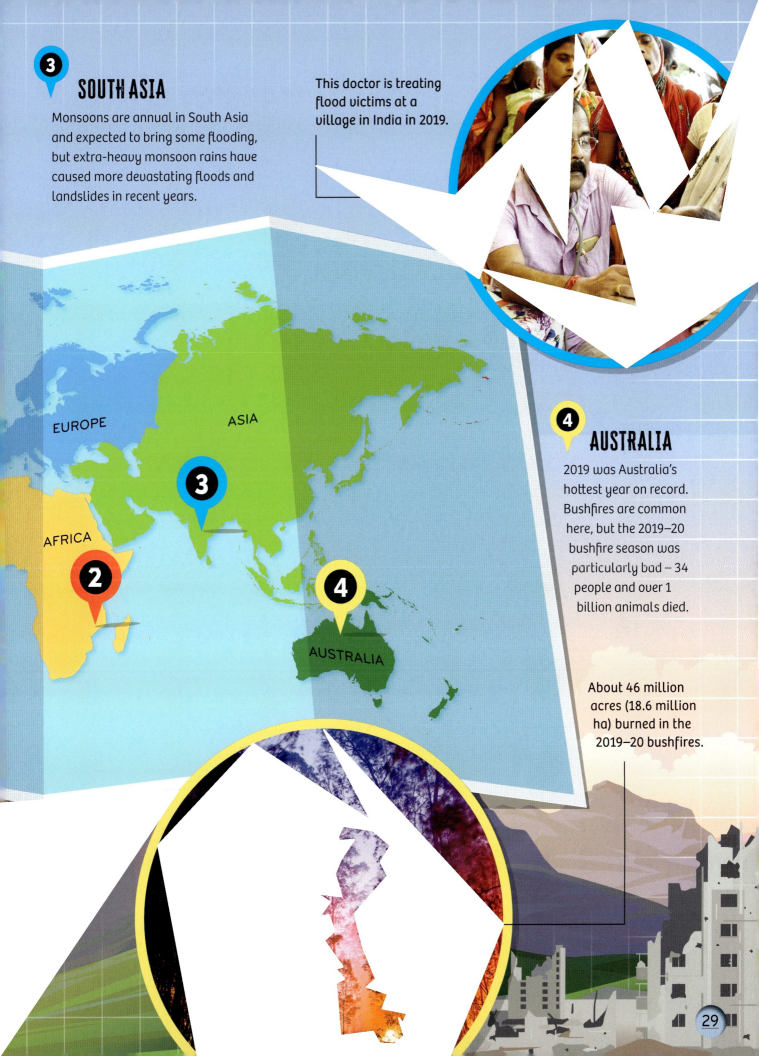

SOUTH ASIA

Monsoons are annual in South Asia and expected to bring some flooding, but extra-heavy monsoon rains have caused more devastating floods and landslides in recent years.

This doctor is treating flood victims at a village in India in 2019.

AUSTRALIA

2019 was Australia's hottest year on record. Bushfires are common here, but the 2019–20 bushfire season was particularly bad – 34 people and over 1 billion animals died.

About 46 million acres (18.6 million ha) burned in the 2019–20 bushfires.

EUROPE

ASIA

AFRICA

AUSTRALIA

GLOSSARY

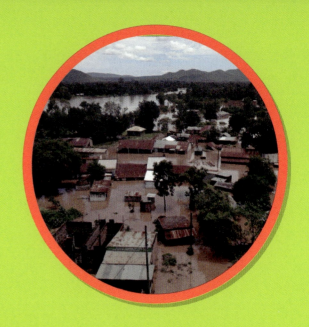

climate change the rising temperature of the Earth's surface and its effects, such as melting ice caps and more extreme weather

crust the outer layer of the Earth

deforestation cutting down trees and clearing the land

desertification when land permanently loses its fertility, so things that grew in the past will no longer grow

displace to move something from its usual place

dormant used to describe a volcano that is not currently active, but is expected to erupt again

ecosystem all the living things in an area and how they affect each other and their environment

erosion when soil is gradually worn away or destroyed, for example by wind or water

evacuate to move people away from a dangerous place

evaporation the process of turning from a liquid into a gas

extinct used to describe a volcano that is unlikely to erupt again

famine a very severe shortage of food in an area

global warming the rising temperature of the Earth's surface; it is caused by very high levels of carbon dioxide and other greenhouse gases in the atmosphere

habitat the place where an animal or plant lives

humanitarian having to do with people's welfare and trying to reduce suffering

magnitude a measure of the size or strength of an earthquake

monsoon a strong seasonal wind that brings heavy rain

pyroclastic flow a very hot, fast-moving flow of lava, ash, and gas

refugee someone who has had to leave their home because of something such as war or famine

saturate to make something thoroughly wet

supervolcano a massive volcano, specifically one that has had an eruption of magnitude 8 on a scale called the Volcano Explosivity Index

tectonics having to do with the structure of the Earth's crust

vegetation all the plants in an area

FURTHER INFORMATION

Books

Earthquakes and **Volcanoes** (Fact Planet) by Izzi Howell (Franklin Watts, 2020)

Hurricanes and Tornadoes and **Wildfires and Freak Weather** (Natural Disaster Zone) by Ben Hubbard (Franklin Watts, 2019)

FICTION
The Long Winter by Laura Ingalls Wilder
Read an incredible account of a winter of extreme blizzards in this book from the **Little House on the Prairie** series. Although this is a storybook, the events in it are based on real life.

Websites

www.open.edu/openlearn/science-maths-technology/wild-weather-kitchen-experiments
Get an adult to help you recreate an avalanche, dust storm, flood, or tornado after watching these "wild weather kitchen experiments".

www.bbc.co.uk/teach/class-clips-video/history-ks4-gcse-what-happened-when-vesuvius-erupted-in-79ad/znww2sg
What happened when Vesuvius erupted in CE 79? Watch this video to find out.

www.natgeokids.com/au/discover/geography/physical-geography/tsunamis
Discover more about tsunamis at this page from National Geographic Kids.

INDEX

Africa 20–21, 22, 23, 28

Australia 24–25, 29

avalanches 4

blizzards 5, 14

climate change 5, 26, 28

cyclones *see* storms

diseases 17, 23

droughts 5, 14, 20, 22–25, 26, 28

earthquakes 4, 7, 10, 11, 12, 13, 16, 17, 27

Egyptians, ancient 18

fires 11, 23, 24, 29

floods 5, 11, 15, 18–21, 26, 29

food 7, 22, 24, 26

Haiti 16–17

hurricanes *see* storms

landslides 11, 21, 29

mudslides 15, 21

poverty 26

Ring of Fire 7

storms 5, 14, 15, 17, 18, 19, 26, 28

tectonic plates 4, 6, 7, 10, 27

tornadoes 5, 14

tsunamis 7, 10, 11
    Indian Ocean tsunami 2004 12–13

volcanoes 4, 6–7, 10, 11, 27
    Vesuvius 8–9

warning systems 9, 13, 19, 26, 27

water 11, 18, 19, 21, 22, 23, 24, 25, 26